Entertaining children has always been my special delight. My own children have children of their own and they are all too old to entertain with chilling tales before bedtime. While awaiting the next generation of giggling offspring, I have decided to put some of these tales in books in case I don't live long enough to deliciously scare them personally.

— Arlo Guthrie

First Edition

Library of Congress Cataloging-in-Publication Data

Guthrie, Arlo

Summary: The story of a boy and his goose, which ends at the family table.

ISBN: 978-0-9915370-6-8

Manufactured in China by C&C Joint Printing Co., (Guang Dong) Ltd. in May 2014

Rising Son International, Ltd.
Washington, MA

Me And My Goose

BY ARLO GUTHRIE
illustrations by Kathy Garren

Rising Son International, Ltd.

me and my goose

ME AND MY PAL

we had some very good times

ME AND MY GOOSE

His name was AL

And he cost only a dime

over mountains we'd stray

PLAYING All DAY

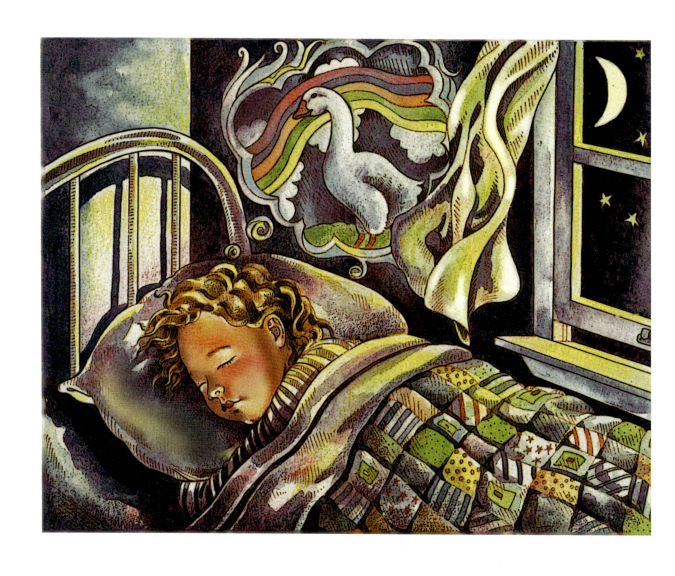

I missed him at Night until Dawn

Then one day I found

He wasn't around

I wondered where Al
could have gone

I looked everywhere

He just wasn't there

Where could a goose be all day?

I MiSS MY PAL

I miss my Al

It's sad that things turned out this way

Then Mom brought him in

I remember her grin

stuffed with his feet pointed straight

I'll never forget

The night that we et

AL off of the old yellow plate